A Dance in the Dark
Book One on Revival:
The Consistency of God

B. J. Isaacs

HarvestNet Publishing

A Dance in the Dark
Book One of *Revival: The Consistency of God*
Copyright © 2017 B. J. Isaacs

Published by HarvestNet Publishing
PO Box 6071, Cleveland, OH 44101

ISBN-13: 9781717431103

All Bible quotations are taken from the *New King James Version*®. Copyright © 1982 by Thomas Nelson. Used by permission. All rights reserved.

All rights reserved. No part of this publication may be reproduced, stored in a retrieval system, or transmitted in any form or by any means – electronic, mechanical, photocopy, recording, or any other – except for brief quotations in printed reviews, without the prior permission of the publisher.
    While the author has made every effort to provide accurate Internet addresses at the time of publication, neither the publisher nor the author assumes any responsibility for errors, or for changes that occur after publication. Further, the publisher does not have any control over and does not assume any responsibility for author or third-party Web sites or their content.

Cover art: Hannah Stari
Interior Art: Christy Isaacs (a.k.a. Jayden Foxx)

Printed in the United States of America

Contents

	Acknowledgments	vii
	Introduction	ix
1	The Dance: Enticement	1
2	From Light to Darkness—	7
3	Step 1: The Dance & Its Consequence	13
4	Step 2: Futile Thoughts & Darkened Hearts	21
5	Recognizing the Dance in the Darkness	41
6	The Ray of Hope—After Darkness, Light	55
7	"One Divine Moment"—A Prayer:	63
	Postlude: The Burden	65
	Bibliography	69
	About the Author	71

Acknowledgments

E. M. Bounds, in his book *Power Through Prayer*, said, "Preaching is not the performance of an hour. It is the outflow of a life. It takes twenty years to make a sermon, because it takes twenty years to make the man" (p. 9). This statement is also abundantly true of the writing of a book. The contents of a book must be the heart and soul of the one who writes the book. A book from the soul is not written in one hour because it has taken a lifetime of God's working into the writer the contents of that book. It is easy to quote other authors, but those quotations may not have searched the depths of the one who is quoting them. However, when a writer has read other authors' works, including the holiest of books, the Bible, and those works have read him, they become the soul and heart of that man.

My longing for revival and the hunger to see God move in this land has been birthed not because I have read many books on revival and prayer, but because many books on revival and prayer have read me. They have shown me my emptiness. They have created a hunger to see the presence of God return to His church in my land. But this in itself would not have caused me to write a book. As I shared my experiences and the things with which God has burdened my heart, again and again people told me that I needed to write a book on revival. There are many books on this subject, but the constant encouragement of others has led to this book.

I am indebted to many. I could use the quote from E. M. Bounds in a different way. I could say, "It takes twenty people to make a book because it takes twenty people to make the man write the book." Many whose names are not listed here greatly influenced the writing of this book by their prayers, insights, and words of encouragement. My gratitude goes out to Daisy E. Bailey and Dana L. Collins from Taylor University. My unplanned meeting with them in Indiana was part of this adventure. I have been encouraged by Rev. Michael Edds, one of my companions in this journey, to seek another revival from God. Rosalie Canfield of Ohio, another divine appointment from God, also encouraged me to write this book. Pastors Bob and Beverly Hils, who are now with the Lord, spoke much into my life. Pastors Joseph and Renee Horevay consistently asked about the progress of the book. Rick and JoAnne Bowser were another couple who were constantly wanting to know about this. Many thanks also to Tom Hare and Steve Neptune of HarvestNet Ministries who provided valuable assistance in getting this book to publication.

I have saved the best for last. This book would not have been completed if not for my wonderful wife, Bonnie, and for Ted Griffin, a friend of many years. You and others are the "twenty" who have written this book.

In spite of all of that, I do not dedicate the book to any particular individual. This book is offered up as a sacrifice to the Lord. May He, through the precious Holy Spirit, use this book as a match in the midst of dry kindling to spark a fire in our nation for His glory.

Introduction

One day the Pharisees and the Sadducees came to test Jesus by asking Him to show them a sign from heaven. The signs of the messianic age were all around them, and yet they wanted Him to prove that He was who He claimed to be. Jesus responded to them by saying, "When it is evening you say, 'It will be fair weather, for the sky is red'; and in the morning, 'It will be foul weather today, for the sky is red and threatening.' Hypocrites! You know how to discern the face of the sky, but you cannot discern the signs of the times" (Matthew 16:2–3). They were students of the Scriptures, but they could not discern the hand of God at work in their generation. (See John 5:39.) They did not understand the ways of God.

It doesn't take a whole lot of discernment to see that things are not going well in our nation and world. Terrorist threats abound, evil is growing, economies are collapsing, and wars and rumors of wars are proliferating. But what seems to be difficult for some to discern is the connection between current events and the great need for revival in the church and in the nation. Divines of the past clearly understood the consequences if God did not send another Great Awakening. John Whitehead, president and founder of the Rutherford Institute, said, "If there isn't a revival in this country of some sort . . . we're moving toward a state that would be very much like pagan Rome" (Duewel, Revival

A Dance in the Dark

Fire, p. 9). Rev. William Gowland once told Colin Whittaker, "It is either revival or revolution for Britain." He then adds, "I believe that applies to America as well as to Britain" (Whittaker, Great Revivals, p 13). The late A.W. Tozer captured the same idea in the title of his book, Rut, Rot or Revival. Would Jesus say of us, "Hypocrites! You can discern the troubled times, but you can't discern the connection between your rebellion against God and the troubled times. Neither can you discern the ways of God in revival to bring repentance and restoration."?

What are the ways of God in revival? The Scriptures and history are filled with them. The problem is, we are disoriented to them. We do not even know the markers, the memorial stones that God has left to show us the way. We do not even hear all of heaven crying out, "Repent and return!" Heaven's cry is drowned out by the cacophony of the world. Revival: The Consistency of God is meant to be a series of smaller books written with the goal of reorienting the church to the ways of God in revival so that we will join Him. These writings are meant to help us become clay in the Potter's hands, so that we might be molded into vessels fit for the Master's use, to draw the Spirit of God into our day, our culture and our time.

Revival: The Consistency of God has come about as a result of a deep soul-searching in my own ministry and the realization of my own powerlessness in the things of God. It is a result of much reading about the revivals of the past and watching movies and videos about them. This research was accompanied by traveling to the gravesides of people whom God used in some of those revivals and some of the

Introduction

places where they occurred. It was birthed through tears because of the realization that the glory of the Lord has departed and we know it not.

Some will say that the premise of this book is false. Some will say that God does not work in such ways. My reply is, just because you have not seen it does not mean that He does not do it or is not doing it. The Pharisees and Sadducees missed what God was doing; He was doing it right under their nose. Revival history and Scripture testify that these are the ways of God in revival. Some will argue that Satan counterfeits. Agreed, but that only proves that the genuine exists as well. If I do not know the ways of God in revival, how can I join Him in his work? Might I not be found to be fighting against what God is doing?

Book One of this series (the book you are reading) is entitled A Dance in the Dark. In this volume we will look at what a culture's dance with darkness looks like and how to recognize it and will look toward God's remedy. We close Book One with a prayer that reflects a heart's cry for God to so move in our time and in our culture as to take us out of darkness into light. Subsequent publications will help us grow in our understanding of what that can look like and how to participate in revival and, by God's grace, intercede and facilitate revival in accord with the consistency of God's character and ways.

Consider with me then, the ways of God in revival, beginning from the vantage point of our position of need.

B. J. Isaacs – January 2017

CHAPTER ONE

THE DANCE: ENTICEMENT

The music played softly as the gentleman held the hands of his beloved. There were no distinguishing characteristics in his appearance. Nothing made Mr. C stand out in a crowd on the dance floor. Nothing made him recognizable except perhaps his plainness and the strange scars upon his hands. In contrast the dance floor was strangely lit—one part flooded with light, the other covered in darkness. Where the light and the darkness met there were graying shadows.

Mr. C's demeanor was calm, gentle, and loving. As he held his beloved close, he whispered to her, "You must never dance in the darkness. There are dangers there." He assured her that if she decided to dance in the darkness, he would never hold her against her will. His love for her would not force her to stay in the well-lit section of the ballroom. He also assured her that if she ever found herself trapped and in the darkness and called to him, he would rescue her.

As the tempo of the music increased, Mr. C took her hand and began to instruct her on how to dance in the light. At times she would stumble or trip over her own feet. Mr. C

A Dance in the Dark

would catch her and steady her balance. He assured her, "You are doing well. Just lean on me. Follow my lead." Just as she was beginning to become accustomed to the dance, out of the corner of her eye she caught a glimpse of a well-groomed, sharply dressed figure of a man standing in the shadows. Although the shadows hid his features, there was something alluring about him and yet alarming at the same time.

At times Mr. C would give her a twirl and then release her hand to give her freedom to spin in the dance. As the dance continued, there were moments when in the free spin she could hear the stranger in the shadows say, "Come dance with me!" Remembering the warning of Mr. C, she would shake her head from side to side signifying that she would not.

Nonetheless, the stranger did not give up. At an opportune moment he would add new enticements. "I can show you steps that he never could. I can introduce you to pleasures that he has never experienced! Come! Dance in the shadows. It's not really dark here. I am a prince. He's just an ordinary man."

As the dance continued, curiosity began to tug at her heart. Could she really find new pleasures in a dance with the stranger? The stranger had assured her that the shadows were not actually dark. On the next pass around the floor when Mr. C let go of her hand, she paused and looked at the outstretched hand of the stranger. The wince upon Mr. C's face told her of his concern. She assured herself that Mr. C said he would not stop her if she wanted to dance in the darkness. She told herself, "I will just dance in the shadows!

What harm could there be in the shadows?" With half a smile she glanced at Mr. C and told herself, "He might be wrong after all."

Taking the hand of the stranger, she began to learn new steps that Mr. C had never taught her. She began to question if Mr. C really knew as much about dancing as he seemed to have known. The new steps with the man in the shadows were intoxicating. Each step made her want more. However, without her realizing it the stranger never let go of her hand as Mr. C had done. This stranger seemed rigid, unrelenting in the accelerating pace. With each increase of the tempo, they were spinning closer and closer to the darkness until finally they were engulfed in the absence of light. She could not see her way. She could not tell what was on the dance floor. The stranger kept saying, "Trust me in the darkness." All she could do was hear the words in her head, "There are dangers there!" And then, as if an echo, "Dangers! Dangers! Dangers!"

The grip of the stranger kept tightening with each spin around the floor. At one point he said to her, "I have you now, my dear, and I will never let you go! I am the prince of this darkness, and this is the dance in the darkness, the dance of doom! Mr. C cannot and will not save you."

Oh, how she wished she had listened to Mr. C.'s warning.

A Dance in the Dark

..Enticement..

The story above is a parable. Mr. C is the Lord Jesus Christ. The beloved lady can represent the life of an individual, a church, or even a nation. As long as we dance in the light with Mr. C, He helps us when we stumble. He encourages us in the dance. But the stranger, the Devil, cannot stand for anyone to dance in the light with Mr. C. The well-dressed stranger, the adversary of our souls, hates the freedom we have when we dance in the light. He wants to entice us to dance the dance of doom in the darkness with him.

I don't know much about dancing, as my wife will attest to you, but I do know there are different types of dances. There are rhumbas, fox-trots, the funky chicken, etc. ...; there are things that make a rhumba a rhumba rather than the twist. However, within each type of dance there may be variations. Even so when a group of people, a culture, or a nation decides to dance in the darkness, certain things mark it as a dance in darkness. Although one nation's dance in

The Dance: Enticement

darkness in history might not have all the marks of another culture's dance in darkness, it is a dance in darkness nonetheless. The dangers of doing the dance of doom in the darkness are very real. Both Scripture and history warn us of the dangers.

Will we heed the warning? Or will we dance to our doom? Will our leaders, both in the church and in government, be like those on the *Titanic* who continued to ignore the warning of the prophets crying, "There is an iceberg ahead"? Do we really believe the ship is unsinkable?

Over the years some have sounded the alarm as they watched the church or a nation slip further and further away from the God of the Bible. In agony and deep concern righteous souls today grieve daily as they watch us spin closer and closer to the unseen danger in the darkness. Some today wonder, "Will we ever come back from the dance near the precipice of doom?"

There is hope, but time is running out.

There is hope, but it is not in our government.

The rays of the light of hope peer over the horizon of the pages of Holy Scripture.

Those rays of hope, like a rock that skips across the water of a pond, do their dance across the centuries of revival history. There we see the flickering flame that remains lit against the gale-force winds of our decadent culture. This hope can be found only in a gracious move of the Spirit of God. Our only hope is in the God of Abraham, Isaac, and Jacob, the Father of our Lord Jesus Christ. In times past God in His great mercy answered the desperate, broken cries of His repentant people who awoke to the fact that

A Dance in the Dark

they were dancing in the darkness. These gracious moves of God were so powerful, wonderful, and dreadful that no man could claim credit for them. This writer has never experienced such a move of God in His entire life. But the pages of revival history and Scripture are filled with them. God has consistently sent these "times of refreshing" (Acts 3:19), and my heart aches as I survey the spiritual barrenness of our land today. In my time alone with God I ask the soul-searching question regarding the evils of our age. "Why could we not cast it out?" (Matthew 17:19).

Where is the power over this increasing darkness? It seems to me that most of the church circles that I have walked in are void of this life-giving power. We are not turning the culture upside down for Jesus. (See Acts 17:6.) If this is not true of you, if this is not true of the portion of the church where you walk and serve, please forgive me, lay this book down, and read no further. If this is not true of you then, please pray for those of us who seem to be in the wilderness. But if you sense the barrenness that I do, if you sense the powerlessness I have described, then ask God to stir deep within you the hope and prayer for a God-sent awakening. This little book (and those that will follow) are not so much a revival history as they are a documentation of a pattern—a consistency that emerges from Scripture and the God–sent revivals of the past. The documentation of this pattern is meant to stir your heart to cry out to God for the "cloud, as small as a man's hand" that signifies the sound of an abundance of rain (1 Kings 18:41-46).

CHAPTER TWO

FROM LIGHT TO DARKNESS—
The Unlearned Lesson:
A Warning to Our Time

Pain and agony come with having to learn over and over again that a dance in the darkness has dire consequences for anyone, whether an individual or a nation. The history of the nation of Israel is filled with the dreadful consequences of its repeated dances in the dark. From its beginning God warned the Israelites during their betrothal period in the wilderness not to dance with anyone but Him. If they decided to switch partners and dance in the darkness, their enemies would rise up against them, and they would not be able to avoid the consequences of the dance. Moses warned the Israelites of these consequences:

> For the LORD your God is a consuming fire, a jealous God. When you beget children and grandchildren and have grown old in the land, act corruptly and make a carved image in the form of anything, and do evil in the sight of the LORD your God to provoke Him to anger…the LORD will scatter you among the peoples, and

> you will be left few in number among the nations where the LORD will drive you…But from there you will seek the LORD your God, and you will find Him if you seek Him with all your heart and with all your soul" (Deuteronomy 4:24–29).

The book of Judges records Israel's repeated decision to leave the arms of the God who loved them. Again and again they chose to sway to the melodic tones of the nations around them who were doing their dance of destruction. Again and again they would break their relationship with God to suffer the consequences of dancing with their elusive, enticing, but deadly partner. Over and over again they would dance in the darkness, only to cry out to God to deliver them from the nightmare of a dance.

It would always start the same way: They would be faithful to God all the days of a leader or leaders who lived during a move of God. "So the people served the LORD all the days of Joshua, and all the days of the elders who outlived Joshua, who had seen all the great works of the LORD which He had done for Israel" (Judges 2:7). As long as the eyewitnesses to the powerful moving of God were alive, the nation followed God.

But as soon as the generation that had witnessed the power of God had died, the people began to listen to the stranger in the darkness. They would be wooed by his enticements to reject God and to embrace the darkness.

> "Now Joshua the son of Nun, the servant of the LORD, died. . . When all that generation had been gathered to their fathers, another generation arose after them who

did not know the LORD nor the work which He had done for Israel. Then the children of Israel did evil in the sight of the LORD, and served the Baals; and they forsook the LORD" (Judges 2:8–12).

When a society or culture forsakes the Lord, God forsakes them (He withdraws His protective power) and turns them over to their enemies.

"They forsook the LORD and served Baal and the Ashtoreths. And the anger of the LORD was hot against Israel. So He delivered them into the hands of plunderers who despoiled them; and He sold them into the hands of all their enemies all around, so that they could no longer stand before their enemies" (Judges 2:13–14; See also Deuteronomy 31:15–18).

It is important to grasp that it is God who causes our armies to be successful or to be defeated. If we abandon Him, we abandon our protection. God then turns us over to be ravaged by our enemies.

Once the tight grip of the enemy (or some other judgment from God) becomes so heavy that the people begin to groan under its weight, the people may or may not turn back to God. If they do turn back to God and begin to cry out to Him, He has promised to hear and to deliver them. From a position of being under the power of the enemy, God promises that if "from there you will seek the LORD your God . . . you will find Him if you seek Him with all your heart and with all your soul" (Deuteronomy 4:29). God promised to hear His people when they cried out to

A Dance in the Dark

Him from that place of humility and desperation. God would then raise up a redeemer, a judge to deliver them out of their oppression.

> "And when the LORD raised up judges for them, the LORD was with the judge and delivered them out of the hand of their enemies all the days of the judge; for the LORD was moved to pity by their groaning because of those who oppressed them and harassed them" (Judges 2:18).

This is also what God meant when He said:

> "When I shut up heaven and there is no rain, or command the locusts to devour the land, or send pestilence among My people, if My people who are called by My name will humble themselves, and pray and seek My face, and turn from their wicked ways, then will I hear from heaven, and will forgive their sin and heal their land" (2 Chronicles 7:13–14).

Unfortunately, God's people did not learn the lesson from the preceding generation and repeated this pattern.

> "And it came to pass, when the judge was dead, that they reverted and behaved more corruptly than their fathers, by following other gods, to serve them and bow down to them. They did not cease from their own doings nor from their stubborn way" (Judges 2:19).

Once Israel abandoned God, the pattern would start all over again.

The Dance & Its Consequence

It is pure folly to think that the warnings given in Scripture to Israel and to other cultures have no application to our time. Paul, in 1 Corinthians 10:6, 11, speaking of what happened to those whom God destroyed in the wilderness because of their rebellion, gives this warning to believers: "Now these things became our examples, to the intent that we should not lust after evil things as they also lusted. . . . Now all these things happened to them as examples, and they are written for our admonition, on whom the ends of the ages have come." Both Jude and Peter give similar warnings. If God judged the angels who decided to dance in the darkness (2 Peter 2:4; Jude 6), if God judged those in the days of Noah who did the dance of doom (2 Peter 2:5), and if God judged those who gave themselves over to sexual immorality in Sodom and Gomorrah (2 Peter 2:6; Jude 7), then we must heed this warning: He will also judge our wickedness.

If in times past God allowed the consequences of choosing to dance in the darkness to come to pass, then what makes us think that we will escape?

CHAPTER THREE

STEP 1:
THE DANCE & ITS CONSEQUENCE
Rejection of Light and
Removal of God's Spirit

Just as physical darkness has certain characteristics, so does a dance in spiritual darkness. What are some of the marks or characteristics of a dance in the darkness?

IT BEGINS WITH REJECTION OF THE LIGHT GOD HAS GIVEN

A dance in spiritual darkness always begins the same way—with the rejection of the one true God or the rejection of His Word. Darkness is the absence of light, whether physical darkness or spiritual darkness. Spiritual darkness exists when God's truth, the light of His word, is suppressed, withheld, or rejected. In our parable the lovely lady rejected the warning from Mr. C. She rejected the notion that dancing in the dark was dangerous. She accepted the idea that the shadows are not really dark. No matter how great or

A Dance in the Dark

how small the light that has been given, a dance in spiritual darkness begins by rejecting that light. Paul, in his letter to believers in Rome, speaks of those in ancient cultures who rejected whatever light God had given them. They "suppress the truth in unrighteousness, because what may be known of God is manifest in them, for God has shown it unto them ... although they knew God, they did not glorify Him as God ... " (Romans 1:18–21). The word "suppress" in this passage means "to push down." Paul then unpacks the description of the consequences that come upon a culture that pushes down the truth of God. When men love darkness rather than light, when men reject God and His truth, the Scriptures and history show that consequences follow.

Ancient pagan cultures are not alone in their rejection of the light that God had given them. As pointed out earlier, the nation of Israel rejected God's light again and again, as demonstrated in the cycles found in the Book of Judges. But Israel continued their rejection beyond the time of the period of the judges. In the days of Ezekiel, God told that prophet:

> "Son of man, I am sending you to the children of Israel, to a rebellious nation that has rebelled against Me; they and their fathers have transgressed against Me to this very day. For they are impudent and stubborn children. I am sending you to them, and you shall say to them, 'Thus says the LORD God.' As for them, whether they hear or whether they refuse—for they are a rebellious house—yet they will know that a prophet has been among them" (Ezekiel 2:3–5).

The Dance & Its Consequence

God told Ezekiel: "But the house of Israel will not listen to you, because they will not listen to Me; for all the house of Israel are impudent and hard-hearted." (Ezekiel 3:7). God was well aware that the children of Israel would reject the words that Ezekiel spoke in His name. However, God sent Ezekiel to warn them anyway.

THE WITHDRAWAL OF THE SPIRIT OF GOD

When truth and light are rejected, God's Spirit begins to withdraw from the culture. It does not happen immediately, but it happens nonetheless. This phenomenon can be seen in different ways in different passages of Scripture, but the consequences are the same.

We have already noted that in Ezekiel's day the people were rebellious and did not wish to hear what God had to say. God had warned Ezekiel that "they and their fathers" (Ezekiel 2:3) would reject the word that He was sending them through Ezekiel. This had been going on for quite a while. What was God's response to this continuous pattern of rejecting His word? It is seen in a slow progression of the manifest glory of God leaving the city of Jerusalem. In Ezekiel 8 the house of God is filled with idols. God brings Ezekiel "to the door of the north gate of the inner court, where the seat of the image of jealousy was, which provokes to jealousy" (v. 3). The inner court is inside the temple. God's manifest presence is still in the temple, but so also is an idol. Ezekiel says "And behold, the glory of the God of Israel was there" (v. 4). In Ezekiel 9:3 we read, "Now the glory of the God of Israel had gone up from the cherub, where it had been, to the threshold of the temple." The Shekinah glory of God had been between the cherubim in the Holy of Holies in the temple, but now it has moved to the threshold of the door. In Ezekiel 10:4 we read, "Then the glory of the LORD went up from the cherub, and paused over the threshold of the temple; and the house was filled with the cloud, and the court was full of the brightness of the LORD's glory." In Ezekiel 10:18–19 we read, "Then the glory of the LORD departed from the threshold of the temple and stood over the cherubim. And the cherubim lifted their wings and mounted up from the earth in my sight." In Ezekiel 11:23 we read, "And the glory of the LORD went up from the midst of the city and stood on the mountain, which is on the east side of the city." After this slow progression of the glory of God leaving the city, God says to Ezekiel, "Son of man, you dwell in the midst of a rebellious house, which has eyes to see but does not see, and ears to hear but does not hear; for they are a rebellious house" (Ezekiel 12:2). God had removed His presence because they refused to listen. They rejected His light and His word to them.

We see in Romans 1 that in the pagan cultures that "suppress the truth in unrighteousness" (v. 18) God withdraws His hand from suppressing evil. Romans 1:24 says, "Therefore God also gave them up to uncleanness, in the lusts of their hearts." God quits restraining the evil in the hearts of those in the culture who suppress His truth. In Romans 1:26 we read, "For this reason God gave them up to vile passions." God turns the culture over to the evil passions that they have. Romans 1:28 adds, "And even as they

The Dance & Its Consequence

did not like to retain God in their knowledge, God gave them over to a debased mind." Cultures that reject the light God has given them end up with debased minds. I submit to you that the decay we see in our culture today is because we have rejected the truth of God. (We will see more of this later on when we look at more of the characteristics of a culture that is doing a dance in the darkness.)

Lest anyone say, "That was then, this is now," lest you think, "God doesn't do that anymore," there is an ominous warning in the writings of the Apostle Paul. Paul, speaking of the Age of Apostasy coming in the end-times, gives a warning to the Church in 2 Thessalonians 2:1–2 not to be shaken or deceived into believing that the Day of the Lord (which is also known as the day of Christ) had already come. He is speaking of the day when Christ returns to gather the church to Himself and to judge the world. Paul then proceeds to give a sequence of things that must occur first. "Let no one deceive you by any means; for that Day will not come unless the falling away comes first" (2 Thessalonians 2:3). The "falling away" spoken of is an apostasy when people reject the truth that God has given and instead embrace darkness. It is during this apostasy that "the man of sin is revealed, the son of perdition, who opposes and exalts himself above all that is called God or that is worshiped, so that he sits as God in the temple of God, showing himself that he is God" (2 Thessalonians 2:3–4). This man is also known as the Antichrist.

Paul makes it clear that something is keeping this from happening yet. Something is keeping the Church and the world as a whole from doing this final dance with darkness.

A Dance in the Dark

"And now you know what is restraining, that he may be revealed in his own time. For the mystery of lawlessness is already at work; only He who now restrains will do so until He is taken out of the way" (2 Thessalonians 2:6–7).

The Antichrist cannot be revealed until "his own time" because Someone is restraining. In the Greek language there are two words for "time"—*chronos* and *kairos*. *Chronos* has to do with chronological time. *Kairos* has to do with a window of opportunity that opens in chronological time. There will be a special window of time in which the Antichrist will have to lure the nations into a final dance of doom in the darkness. Until that time comes, Someone is restraining the Antichrist from taking over. That Someone is the Holy Spirit. But once the Holy Spirit is "taken out of the way" "the lawless one will be revealed, whom the Lord will consume with the breath of His mouth and destroy with the brightness of His coming" (2 Thessalonians 2:7–8).

But how is the lawless one going to gain power and popularity? How is he going to seduce people to do the dance of doom? "The coming of the lawless one is according to the working of Satan, with all power, signs, and lying wonders, and with all unrighteous deception among those who perish, because they did not receive the love of the truth, that they might be saved" (2 Thessalonians 2:9–10). Because they did not receive the love of the truth, "for this reason God will send them strong delusion, that they should believe the lie, that they all may be condemned who did not believe the truth but had pleasure in unrighteousness" (2 Thessalonians 2:11–12).

Why will the Holy Spirit be removed at the end of the

The Dance & Its Consequence

age? People will reject the truth of God, and as a result God will move the Holy Spirit out of the way and send them a delusion so that they believe a lie. They will be deceived by the greatest deceiver of all time. They will accept the Antichrist as being God in human flesh. They will do a dance with the Great Pretender. And they will all be condemned. They will ignore the warning to not dance in the darkness, will take the hand of the Antichrist, and will twirl away to their doom.

Both Holy Scripture and history beyond the pages of Scripture strike the notes and chords of the discordant dance of a nation's demise. From the pages of the Bible and history let us seek to compose the strophes in the dance of a nation for whom a funeral requiem will play.

THEY ABANDON THE WORD, THE LIGHT OF GOD, THE TRUTH

We have previously looked at the nation of Israel's history of rejecting God's Word, Paul's references in Romans 1 about pagan nations that suppressed the truth of God, and Paul's warnings about the end-times when whole nations will reject the truth, believe a lie, and follow the Antichrist. It is important to stress that this is the case with every nation and culture that has done, and is doing, the dance of doom.

This was true with King Jehoiakim who sliced up the word of God that was sent to him by Jeremiah and threw it into the fire because he did not like what it said (Jeremiah 36:1–26).

It was true with Adolf Hitler and the Third Reich. Alt-

A Dance in the Dark

hough Hitler belonged to the Church, he was not a true believer in Jesus Christ. The Church was simply used by him as a tool, and he did all he could to change it and bring about his agenda. "According to Hitler, Christianity preached 'meekness and flabbiness, and this was simply not useful to the National Socialist ideology, which preached 'ruthlessness and strength.' In time, he felt that the churches would change their ideology. He would see to it" (Eric Metaxas, *Bonhoeffer*, p. 166). All who bring their culture or nation into a dance in the darkness will work to change the Church's ideology, its historical doctrines. Many of those who surrounded Hitler "were bitterly anti-Christian and were ideologically opposed to Christianity, and wanted to replace it with a religion of their own devising." Under their leadership, said William L. Shirer, "the Nazi regime intended eventually to destroy Christianity in Germany, if it could, and substitute the old paganism of early tribal Germanic gods, and the new paganism of the Nazi extremists" (quoted in Metaxas, *Bonhoeffer*, p. 169). Like the pagan nations mentioned by Paul in Romans 1, the Nazis rejected the truth and the light of God's Word. They wished to replace it with their own ideas. The Nazis led Germany into a dance in the darkness with all the consequences that followed.

What will the end be for our beloved nation as we see the truth being rejected more and more in this land of ours? We have begun the dance in the darkness to the melody of the dirge. Do we not see many who hate Christianity now surround some of our leaders? Do we not see Biblical ideas being replaced with the new ones of the enlightened elite?

CHAPTER FOUR

STEP 2: FUTILE THOUGHTS & DARKENED HEARTS

As the light of God is rejected, the people and the leaders of the nation develop futile thoughts and darkened hearts. Romans 1:21 says, ". . . because, although they knew God, they did not glorify Him as God, nor were thankful, but became futile in their thoughts, and their foolish hearts were darkened." These futile thoughts and darkened hearts play themselves out in many aspects of the society and culture.

Several things come about with twisted thinking and darkened hearts.

SOMETHING ELSE BECOMES GOD: (EVIL RULERS COME TO POWER

Once the Holy Spirit begins His withdrawal from a culture, once God begins to turn them over to a reprobate mind (see Ezekiel and Romans 1), once God stops restraining the evil (2 Thessalonians 2), the thinking of the culture becomes more and more twisted. "Professing to be wise, they became fools" (Romans 1:22). They "exchanged the truth of God for the lie, and worshiped and served the creature rather than the Creator, who is blessed forever" (Romans 1:25).They begin to worship something or someone other than the one true God. They might begin to worship literal idols, or they might begin to worship someone, sometimes themselves. For ancient Rome, the Caesars became gods. In ancient Babylon, Nebuchadnezzar made a statue of gold and demanded that everyone worship it (Daniel 3). In Hitler's Germany it was the intent of leaders of the Nazi party to make Hitler a god. Reinhard Heydrich, one of the leaders of the Third Reich, at one time proclaimed, "You'll see the day, ten years from now, when Adolf Hitler will occupy precisely the same position in Germany that Jesus Christ has now" (Metaxas, *Bonhoeffer*, p. 170). Hitler was to replace Christ.

What is beginning to take the place of Jesus Christ in our nation? What is taking the place of His truth?

SEXUAL IMMORALITY AND CASTING OFF MORAL RESTRAINT BECOMES THE NORM

A culture that is dancing in darkness becomes sexually aberrant. A culture that is doing the dance of doom begins to practice all kinds of sexual deviations from God's norm. God's only norm for sexual relations is inside the bonds of holy matrimony—namely, one man and one woman for life. Any other form of sexual gratification is outside of God's norm. It does not matter whether it is pornography, bestiality, bisexuality, homosexuality (even monogamous), adultery, fornication, pederasty, or any other form of sexual gratifica-

Step 2: Futile Thoughts & Darkened Hearts

tion. In our day there have been many attempts to justify same-sex marriage by attacking the traditional interpretations of Genesis 19, 1 Corinthians 6:9–11, and other passages. However, Jesus defined marriage in Matthew 19:1–10. The context of this Biblical passage deals with divorce, but Jesus clearly saw marriage as based on a male and female relationship, asking His challengers, "Have you not read that He who made them at the beginning 'made them male and female'?" and He added, "'For this reason a man shall leave his father and mother and be joined to his wife, and the two shall become one flesh.'" We must not miss the connection between the rejection of God's light and truth on marriage and the increase in sexual immorality. Jesus continued, "And I say to you, whoever divorces his wife, except for sexual immorality, and marries another, commits adultery." We must not miss the point that to focus on homosexuality alone is to miss the overall teaching of Scripture. A culture doing the dance of doom is sexually deviant in many ways.

All the men in the town of Sodom had become sexually perverse. When Lot had urged the two angels (who had come in the appearance of men) to not spend the night in the town square, "The men of the city, the men of Sodom, both old and young, all the people from every quarter, surrounded the house. And they called to Lot and said to him, 'Where are the men who came to you tonight? Bring them out to us that we may know them carnally" (Genesis 19:4–5). I understand that the word "carnally" is not in the original text, but this was not an innocent request to say, "Hi! Who are you?" It was a demand for Lot to surrender the men to be raped by the whole town of men. That is the only logical explanation for Lot's offering his two virgin daughters to them. Needless to say, the men of Sodom did not want the women; they only wanted the men. Some have suggested that God's judgment came on Sodom and Gomorrah because they intended to gang rape the two angels. That misses the point that the place was sexually deviant and that God had already intended to judge this wicked culture before that incident ever occurred. Others use Ezekiel 16:49 to say that the sin of Sodom was not sexual in nature, but that passage is actually referring to the spiritual condition of Samaria and Jerusalem. Again I stress that if we focus only on homosexuality in this discussion, we will miss the point. <u>A nation or culture that is doing a dance in the darkness is sexually deviant in many aspects.</u>

In Romans 1 we are clearly told regarding those "who suppress the truth in unrighteousness" that "God gave them up to vile passions. For even their women exchanged the natural use for what is against nature. Likewise also the men, leaving the natural use of the woman, burned in their lust for one another, men with men committing what is shameful, and receiving in themselves the penalty of their error which was due" (vv. 26–27). It is clear that this text is about homosexuality and is not about male temple prostitutes. That concept is a recent revisionist construct. But again we must not miss the point that the text is not only about homosexuality. The broader text includes many other sins. The whole culture is doing a dance in darkness.

Judges 19 tells about men asking to sexually molest a man but being just as content to take the women. Here we

Step 2: Futile Thoughts & Darkened Hearts

have a case of bisexuals. God had warned the Israelites when they came out of Egypt, "You shall not lie with a male as with a woman. It is an abomination" (Leviticus 18:22). This text could not be clearer. This text is not about temple male prostitutes. A nation or culture that rejects God will become sexually immoral in many areas (Romans 1:28–29).

RULERS LEAD THE PEOPLE ASTRAY, INTO IMMORALITY AND MORE REJECTION OF GOD

The morality of the people sinks into depravity because of evil rulers. God's accusation against King Ahaz of Israel was, "For the LORD brought Judah low because of Ahaz king of Israel, for he had encouraged moral decline in Judah and had been continually unfaithful to the LORD" (2 Chronicles 28:19). Do we grasp the severity of this statement? God brings nations low when their leaders lead the people into moral decline. Many of our leaders both in the Church and in the government are leading our nation into the acceptance of the homosexual lifestyle. They push transgender bathroom bills. They push the murder of children in the womb. Cohabitation is encouraged. They encourage moral decline in many ways.

The Bible is clear that God raises up rulers and puts them down. In a culture that is doing a dance in the darkness, the leaders begin to lead the nation away from God. Those leaders may even have been put in their position of power by God. In the northern tribes of Israel God had raised to power a man by the name of Baasha. God at one point rebuked him: "Inasmuch as I lifted you out of the dust and made you ruler over My people Israel, and you have walked in the way of Jeroboam, and have made My people Israel sin, to provoke Me to anger with their sins, surely I will take away the posterity of Baasha and the posterity of his house, and I will make your house like the house of Jeroboam the son of Nebat" (1 Kings 16:2–3).

Make no mistake about it—wicked leaders provoke God to anger. God said of wicked King Ahab, "Ahab did more to provoke the LORD God of Israel to anger than all the kings of Israel who were before him" (1 Kings 16:33). There are consequences both to the people and to the leaders who lead the people into a dance in darkness.

LEADERS ENACT LAWS CONTRARY TO THE WAYS OF GOD

Romans 1:32 condemns those who not only do wickedness but approve those who practice such evils.

The Bible book of Daniel (chapter 3) tells the story of King Nebuchadnezzar who made a golden idol and demanded that everyone bow down to it and worship it. The penalty for not doing so was death. It didn't matter what your religious convictions were; it was bow or die. Our land is already being filled with those who are paying a price for refusing to bow to the political correctness of this generation. Baronella Stutzman was fined for refusing to use her gifting from God to make flower arrangements for a gay wedding. The Benham brothers lost their HGTV show because of their Biblical stance on traditional marriage. Many more could be named. The darkness is growing.

Step 2: Futile Thoughts & Darkened Hearts

Laws are being made that oppress followers of God to make them conform to something ungodly. Caesars of Rome demanded that they be worshipped. King Darius in the book of Daniel was tricked into making a law that no one could pray or make a request to any person or god except him for thirty days. The penalty was to be thrown into the lion's den. The deceptiveness of the enemy in singling out those with whom they are at odds comes in all forms. Sometimes their way of finding out who you are may even be disguised as proudly showing your heritage. "On September 15, 1935, the Nuremberg laws were announced" (Metaxas, *Bonhoeffer*, p. 280). These laws were intended to protect the German bloodline. However, among these laws was one that stated, "Jews are forbidden to display the Reichsflagge or the national colors. On the other hand they are permitted to display the Jewish colors. The exercise of this right is protected by the state" (Metaxas, *Bonhoeffer*, p. 280). There is nothing quite as clever as putting a flag out (under the guise of your "right" to do so) and thus alerting those who hate you and want to do you harm exactly where you are! What devious ways might be being contrived to mark those who refuse to bow to the golden idols of our own politically correct age?

THE CULTURE BEGINS TO PERSECUTE ANYONE WHO SPEAKS TRUTH: PEOPLE BECOME AFRAID TO SPEAK THE TRUTH

There are many Scriptural examples of this chord in the funeral requiem of a culture doing its dance of doom, but perhaps the account of a meeting between Elijah and Oba-

A Dance in the Dark

diah, the servant of King Ahab (found in 1 Kings 18), illustrates it best. Ahab and Jezebel had brought Baal worship to Israel, creating a supposedly inclusive society—inclusive to all except those who disagreed with them. They sought to kill any of God's prophets who might point out any of their faulty thinking. Elijah had prophesied drought upon the land due to the wickedness of Ahab and the people. The nation was running out of water and grass for the livestock. Ahab needed to find some. So Ahab said to Obadiah, "Go into the land to all the springs of water and to all the brooks; perhaps we may find grass to keep the horses and mules alive, so that we will not have to kill any livestock" (1 Kings 18:5). While on this quest, Obadiah runs into Elijah. Elijah tells Obadiah to go and tell Ahab that he is coming to meet him. Obadiah's immediate response is one of fear: "How have I sinned, that you are delivering your servant into the hand of Ahab, to kill me? . . . Was it not reported to my lord what I did when Jezebel killed the prophets of the LORD, how I hid one hundred men of the LORD's prophets, fifty to a cave, and fed them with bread and water?" (vv. 9, 13). Obadiah had risked his life to try and hide prophets of the Lord because Jezebel and Ahab wanted to silence all the ministers who might dare to speak the truth in the public square and speak out against Ahab and Jezebel. There was freedom of speech—as long as you didn't disagree with the ruling powers! That is what happens in a culture that is doing a dance with doom.

Likewise, a culture doing a dance with doom will not only seek to silence any who speak truth—it will create an atmosphere of fear to keep the populace in line so that they

Step 2: Futile Thoughts & Darkened Hearts

will not respond to the truth. We see this in the account of Elijah on top of Mount Carmel. When Elijah had gathered Ahab, the false prophets, and all the people on top of Mount Carmel, Elijah issued an open challenge to the people in the form of a question: "How long will you falter between two opinions? If the LORD is God, follow Him; but if Baal, follow him" (1 Kings 18:21a). So hostile was the environment to truth that the people were afraid to openly respond to Elijah's call to come to truth, to the one true God. The following words are some of the saddest in this story: "But the people answered him not a word" (1 Kings 18:21 b). In a culture that is doing a dance of doom, as long as you are in agreement with the powerful elite you have freedom of speech, but woe unto you if you dare speak the truth. People fear for their lives, hesitating to even respond to a call to truth and to the one true God.

LEADERS, SEEKING TO SOLVE THE CULTURE'S WOES, EMBRACE THE VERY THINGS THAT BRING MORE OF GOD'S JUDGMENTS

In a culture dancing the dance of doom, leaders develop twisted thinking. In seeking to solve the cultures woes, they embrace as a means of deliverance from the woes, things that bring God's judgments. In 2 Chronicles 28:22–23 we read: "Now in the time of his distress King Ahaz became increasingly unfaithful to the LORD. This is that King Ahaz. For he sacrificed to the gods of Damascus which had defeated him, saying, 'Because the gods of the kings of Syria help them, I will sacrifice to them that they may help me.' But they were the ruin of him and all Israel." Ahaz was the king of Judah and "had encouraged moral decline" in the nation (2 Chronicles 28:19). When a leader of a nation encourages moral decline, the result for the nation will not be good. As a result of Ahaz's actions he was facing military troubles on every side (2 Chronicles 28:16–21). He tried to get help from other nations rather than turning to the Lord. Since he could not get the help he wanted, he came up with another plan. He decided to adopt the worship of the nation that had defeated him. Brilliant idea? No! He had abandoned the one true God who could help him. He now did the unthinkable. He embraced a foreign god that the one true God had promised would only bring defeat and more of the judgments of God (see Deuteronomy 30:17–18). What current policies or practices are the leaders of our land embracing that they think will bring success, but in fact will bring the judgments of God?

CHILDREN ARE NOT VALUED AND ARE SACRIFICED TO WHATEVER THE CULTURE IS WORSHIPPING

In a culture dancing in the darkness, life is not valued, and relationships within the family become strained. Consider the last warning that God gave to Israel before God became silent for four hundred years. In the Book of Malachi, God reveals what the ministry of the coming Elijah would be: "And he will turn the hearts of the fathers to the children, and the hearts of the children to their fathers, lest I come and strike the earth with a curse" (Malachi 4:6). Part of the coming Elijah's ministry was to help mend family relationships. That is because in a culture that is doing the dance of doom, family relationships are shattered. God clearly warns

Step 2: Futile Thoughts & Darkened Hearts

that unless family relationships are mended a curse will necessarily follow. A culture doing a dance of doom does not value the original God-established family structure.

In such a culture children become disobedient to their parents (Romans 1:30). In such a culture children's lives are not even valued. This can be seen in the life of King Ahaz: "He burned incense in the valley of the son of Hinnom, and burned his children in the fire, according to the abominations of the nations whom the LORD had cast out before the children of Israel" (2 Chronicles 28:3–5).

What he hoped to gain was more important to him than the lives of his own children. This passage is also a reminder that God destroys nations that destroy their children. God brought Israel against the nations that had practiced these things. This can also be seen in Hiel of Bethel who "built Jericho. He laid its foundation with Abiram his firstborn, and with his youngest son Segub he set up its gates" (1 Kings 16:34). This a reference to the fact that he literally sacrificed them in order to rebuild a city that had been cursed. How many of our children will we sacrifice to rebuild or gain something that God has cursed? How many more children will we sacrifice on our altars to Baal (we call it abortion) to defend a twisted concept of women's rights? There is a Biblically correct way of treating and viewing women with respect.

ENTERTAINMENT BECOMES DARK, TWISTED AND SENSUAL

The Apostle Paul in Galatians 5 draws a contrast between the lifestyle of those who walk in the Spirit and those who

A Dance in the Dark

do the works of the flesh. This contrast is applicable to cultures as well. The more people there are in a culture who are walking in the Spirit, the more godly the culture will be. The more people in a culture who are following the works of the flesh, the more ungodly the culture will become. Notice the outworking of a culture that is doing a dance in the darkness because their thinking is futile:

> "Now the works of the flesh are evident, which are: adultery, fornication, uncleanness, lewdness, idolatry, sorcery, hatred, contentions, jealousies, outbursts of wrath, selfish ambitions, dissensions, heresies, envy, murders, drunkenness, revelries, and the like; of which I tell you beforehand, just as I also told you in time past, that those who practice such things will not inherit the kingdom of God" (Galatians 5:19–21).

Notice the ways in which people fill their time when the culture is doing a dance of doom. There is an increase in sexual deviancy: "fornication, uncleanness, lewdness." Later in this list we find "drunkenness, revelries." These all refer to a party lifestyle. The ways people entertain themselves becomes increasingly dark. This can easily be expanded to include theaters and other forms of entertainment. It stands to reason that the more people there are like this in a culture, the more engulfed the culture becomes in these things. There is an increase in our culture through various forms of media to participate in ways to watch bloodshed.

THE PARTY LIFE RUES WHILE GOD'S JUDGMENTS ARE STANDING AT THE DOOR

Step 2: Futile Thoughts & Darkened Hearts

One of the most bizarre aspects of a culture that is doing this dance of doom is that people begin to think they are invincible. They begin to think that no one is able to defeat them. They think that God will not judge them. This attitude can be seen in the words of the nation of Edom. God warned that nation, "The pride of your heart has deceived you, you who dwell in the clefts of the rock, whose habitation is high; you who say in your heart, 'Who will bring me down to the ground?'"(Obadiah 3). Edom had a virtual impenetrable fortress in the clefts of a mountain. They thought no one could conquer them. They thought they were the most powerful nation on the face of the earth. But God warned them, "'Though you ascend as high as the eagle, and though you set your nest among the stars, from there I will bring you down,' says the LORD" (Obadiah 4). Many other nations noted in Scripture had this same arrogance. In Isaiah 14 it was the nation of Babylon. In Jeremiah 49 it was the Ammonites. In Jeremiah 21 it was God's own people, the nation of Judah with its capital at Jerusalem. A nation that persistently forsakes God is headed for judgment. Consider God's warning to Judah: "I will utter My judgments against them concerning all their wickedness, because they have forsaken Me, burned incense to other gods, and worshiped the works of their own hands" (Jeremiah 1:16). Consider also Psalm 9:17: "The wicked shall be turned into hell, and all the nations that forget God." When a nation abandons God, judgments come. There are many purposes for God's judgments. God's overall intent is not to destroy but to turn a people from their wicked ways. This can be seen in 2 Chronicles 7:13–14: "When I shut up heaven and there is no rain, or command the locusts to devour the land, or send pestilence among My people, if My people who are called by My name will humble themselves, and pray and seek My face, and turn from their wicked ways, then I will hear from heaven, and will forgive their sin and heal their land." The purpose of the judgments in verse 14 was to get the people to "turn from their wicked ways"—repentance—so that God would heal their land.

However, if a people refuse to repent, the judgments will increase. This is shown in the prophet Amos. In Amos 4:2–6 God tells Israel about their sins and the judgment that He sent. What was their response? "'Yet you have not returned to Me,' says the LORD" (Amos 4:6). So in Amos 4:7–8, God discusses another judgment that He sent upon them. What was their response to this set of judgments? "'Yet you have not returned to Me,' says the LORD" (Amos 4:8). So in Amos 4:9 God tells of another judgment that He sent. Did this cause them to repent? Again God says, "'Yet you have not returned to Me,' says the LORD." This repeats itself two more times in Amos 4:10–11. Finally God says in an ominous statement, "Therefore thus I will do to you, O Israel; because I will do this to you, prepare to meet your God, O Israel!" (Amos 4:12).When all the judgments do not bring the desired effect, God says, "Prepare to meet Me!" The judgments become one judgment after another, unrelenting judgments.

This concept is seen in several passages of Scripture. God warned Israel through Ezekiel, "Destruction comes; they will seek peace, but there shall be none. Disaster will come upon disaster, and rumor will be upon rumor. Then

Step 2: Futile Thoughts & Darkened Hearts

they will seek a vision from a prophet; but the law will perish from the priest, and counsel from the elders" (Ezekiel 7:25–26). God warned Jerusalem, "They will go out from one fire, but another fire will devour them" (Ezekiel 15:7). In Amos it is described this way: "It will be as though a man fled from a lion, and a bear met him; or as though he went into the house, leaned his hand on the wall, and a serpent bit him." (Amos 5:19). There will be calamities everywhere without escape. People will seek answers from the prophets and priests, but there will be none. There will be a deafening silence in heaven and from heaven. Could the "silence in heaven for about half an hour" (Revelation 8:1) be God listening to hear if any will repent before He sends the judgments found in the seven trumpets? God waits for people to repent, but when they do not, the judgments intensify.

The most perplexing part of this is that with the judgments of God increasing in the land because of increasing sin and evil, people ignore the warnings of the prophets of God. They refuse to repent and turn from their wicked ways. They act as if nothing is wrong. As a matter of fact they party away with the judgments going on all around them. The prophet Amos and the prophet Isaiah both give a picture of this phenomenon.

In Amos 4 we have already seen God telling Israel that they refused to repent even with all of His judgments coming upon them. In Amos 6 God begins a repudiation of the mind-set of His own people. In Amos 6:1–2 God takes them to task for thinking that He will not judge them. "Woe to you who are at ease in Zion, and trust in Mount Samaria, notable persons in the chief nation, to whom the house of

A Dance in the Dark

Israel comes!" Judgments are all around them, but they are at ease. They trust in Mount Samaria. They think they are invincible. They believe that God will not allow their destruction in spite of their rebellion against Him. God quickly points out to them other cultures He has destroyed because of their wickedness: "Go over to Calneh, and see; and from there go to Hamath the great; then go down to Gath of the Philistines. Are you better than these kingdoms? Or is their territory greater than your territory?" Judgment is all around, but they think it won't overtake them.

Then in the midst of all of this God says something to them that is shocking. He rebukes them for partying as if the day of doom is not near.

> "Woe to you who put far off the day of doom, who cause the seat of violence to come near; who lie on beds of ivory, stretch out on your couches, eat lambs from the flock and calves from the midst of the stall; who sing idly to the sound of stringed instruments, and invent for yourselves musical instruments like David; who drink wine from bowls, and anoint yourselves with the best ointments, but are not grieved for the affliction of Joseph. Therefore they shall now go captive as the first of the captives, and those who recline at banquets shall be removed" (Amos 6:3–7).

The picture here is a banqueting feast going on while the signs of God's judgments are all around them.

Through the prophet Isaiah, the Lord gives the same warning. In Isaiah 5:8 God tells about some of the excessive practices of the people of Judah: "Woe to those who join

Step 2: Futile Thoughts & Darkened Hearts

house to house, who add field to field, till there is no place where they may dwell alone in the midst of the land!" They are so busy accumulating things that there is no space or place for quiet solitude. In Isaiah 5:9–10 God then tells of the judgment that will come upon them. In Isaiah 5:11–12 God addresses their partying attitude while judgment is at the door: "Woe to those who rise early in the morning, that they may follow intoxicating drink; who continue until night, till wine inflames them! The harp and the strings, the tambourine and flute, and wine are in their feasts; but they do not regard the work of the LORD, nor consider the operation of His hands." The work being referred to is the work of God's judgments all around them because of their wickedness. Instead of repentance, they party on. As a matter of fact in Isaiah 5:18 God speaks of the heaviness of their sin as being pulled around with cords of emptiness. In Isaiah 5:19 they mock the warning of God's judgments: They "say, 'Let Him make speed and hasten His work, that we may see it; and let the counsel of the Holy One of Israel draw near and come, that we may know it.'" In Isaiah 5:20 they "call evil good, and good evil." In Isaiah 5:21 they are "wise in their own eyes." What folly! But this is a picture of the twisted thinking of a culture that is doing the dance of doom.

VIOLENCE AND BLOODSHED INCREASE

Romans 1:29 speaks of the streets and open squares not being safe. In Genesis 19 when the two angels came to Sodom, Lot invited them into his house. The angels stated,

A Dance in the Dark

"We will spend the night in the open square" (v. 2). Lot was well aware of how unsafe that decision would be. So "he insisted strongly; so they turned in to him and entered his house" (v. 3). The town had become so sexually perverted from its dance in the darkness that Lot knew that the open town square was not safe.

Judges 19 records a similar story. A Levite and his concubine entered Gibeah. He sat down in the open square because no one would take them into their house to spend the night. Finally an old man came by and "saw the traveler in the open square of the city" (v. 17). The old man's advice to the Levite was, "Do not spend the night in the open square" (v. 20). The old man understood how dark the town had become. (Here, as previously referenced, the sexual perversion involved bisexuals who were as willing to rape women as to rape men.)

Look again at Romans 1:29–31 and consider the litany of evil that makes streets unsafe in a culture that is doing a dance of doom: "being filled with all unrighteousness, sexual immorality, wickedness, covetousness, maliciousness; full of envy, murder, strife, deceit, evil-mindedness; they are whisperers, backbiters, haters of God, violent, proud, boasters, inventors of evil things, disobedient to parents, undiscerning, untrustworthy, unloving, unforgiving, unmerciful." All of this leads to more and more violence and unsafe streets. It leads to disrespect for law and order. Note also that the red horse in Revelation 6 portrays the judgment of God which manifests in violence and bloodshed.

The Educational System Seeks to Remove Any Vestige of the One True God, Preparing People to Function in This World But Not for the Next

The greatest example of this is found in the book of Daniel. When Nebuchadnezzar captured Jerusalem and carried the people of Judah into captivity, they changed the godly names of people to names that reflected the values of Babylon. The new names were intended to make them forget their heritage. They insisted upon the captives learning to eat the things that were contrary to their culture. They even demanded that the captives worship the gods of Babylon. When a culture is doing its dance of doom, its leaders will seek to destroy any godly foundation that exists. They will use the educational system to accomplish that task.

CHAPTER FIVE

RECOGNIZING THE DANCE IN THE DARKNESS

Up to this point I have been seeking to strike the notes that are played in the melody of a culture that is doing a dance in the dark. I have covered fourteen characteristics of a culture that is doing the dance of doom. I sought to do this by painting a word picture of patterns that repeat themselves in such a dance. Not every culture that is doing this dance displays all of them. There are also characteristics that I have not covered. In a culture that is doing this dance, the people of God are sometimes weak and powerless against the forces of evil because they have become like the culture around them.

What follows is an exercise to see how well you have learned what a dance in the darkness looks and sounds like. The tune of the dance of doom has repeated itself throughout different cultures and different time periods in history. Can you recognize it from the examples below? Even small snippets of history display some of these characteristics.

A Dance in the Dark

ASSIGNMENT

Read: The nine sections of history listed below are described in the exercise that follows.
1) Florence, Italy—late 1480's.
2) England—1647.
3) England—1660's to early 1700's.
4) United States—1730's to 1740's.
5) United States—1790's to 1835.
6) Wales—1858–1859.
7) South Wales—1859.
8) North Wales—1859–1860.
9) Northern Ireland—1920's.

List: As your read each section of history, whether a lengthy section or a short one, list on a piece of paper the characteristics of the dance in the darkness that you see in that period of history. Perhaps you will recognize some that have not even been mentioned in this book.

Compare: At the end of the nine different time periods you will find my list. Compare yours with mine. You may have some that I do not have. I may have some that you do not.

Apply: Go one step further. Can you recognize different tones of the dance of doom that is going on where you live? Is your culture doing a dance in the darkness to the melody of doom? What truths have you learned?

FLORENCE, ITALY—LATE 1480's

James Gilchrist Lawson in his book *Deeper Experiences of*

Recognizing the Dance in the Darkness

Famous Christians writes, "The Renaissance, or revival of learning, had affected Florence more than any other city. The De Medici had done much to make it a learned and cultured city, and most of the people knew Greek and Latin and could read the classics." Thus you would expect "to find the Florentines leading purer and nobler lives than those of other cities." That is, if you believe that education and culture change the soul of a man. But instead in Florence, Italy in that day, "beneath the veneer of learning the people were utterly corrupt, and . . . they were given over to shows, festivals, worldly display, and entertainments. They were dissolute (lacking restraint, loose in conduct and morals), selfish, pleasure-loving, and had but little thought about God or spiritual things" (Lawson, p. 77). "The luxury, splendor and wealth displayed by the rich in contrast with the awful poverty of the lowly peasants weighed heavily. . . Italy was the prey of petty tyrants and wicked priests, and dukes and popes who strived with each other for political power and control" (David Smithers, *Girolamo Savonarola: Prayer Makes History*).

ENGLAND—1647

In England in 1647 "the churches were for the most part dead and bound in man-made traditions and formalism. When the Church drifts into formalism, the world drifts into further ungodliness" (David Smithers, *George Fox: Prayer Makes History*). In Kidderminster, England in 1647 there was ". . . a population of about 3000 weavers who were reckless, ungodly and content to remain that way. . . Dr. Bates reported that 'The place before his coming was like a piece of dry and barren earth.'" J.C. Ryle said of this time "ministers were wrangling about the divine right of Episcopacy or Presbytery, or splitting hairs about reprobation and free-will ... others were entangling themselves in politics..." (David Smithers, *Richard Baxter: Prayer Makes History*)

ENGLAND—LATE 1660's To EARLY 1700's

According to Winkie Pratney, Arnold Dallimore, in his book on George Whitefield, described this time period as follows:

> In the violent rejection of Puritanism that accompanied the Restoration of the English monarchy, much of the nation threw off restraint and plunged into godlessness, drunkenness, immorality and gambling. Puritans became a thorn in the side of the State church and faced increasing legal hassle. Finally in 1662 nearly 2,000 ministers—all who would not submit to an Act of Uniformity—were ejected from their churches. Forbidden to preach under severe penalties, many, like John Bunyan, imprisoned, hundreds suffered and some died. Then *Deism* rose in the nation from 1660 to 1670, a vicious thought-war against supernatural Christianity, seeking to rationalize everything; the Bible, the virgin birth, miracles (pp. 65–66).

Deism was a false belief system that said human reason rather than divine revelation is the way to reach morality and truth. It denied that the creator was any longer involved with the laws of the universe. Dallimore continues:

Recognizing the Dance in the Darkness

> Of course the Church responded, but with coldly correct apologetics that lacked soul and fire. Large numbers, both high and low class, dropped out of the church believing Christianity to be false. Religion became ritual; the people above all feared 'enthusiasm'—anyone whose practice of Christianity showed any true fervor. Empty formality was the order of the day (pg. 66).

In further description of the times, Dallimore said:

> ...the Gin Craze began in 1689, and within a generation every 6th house became a gin shop. The poor were unspeakably wretched—over 160 crimes had the death penalty! Gin made the people what they never were before—cruel and inhuman. Hanging was a daily gala event; those jerking on ropes were watched and applauded by men, women and children who crowded the gallows for the best view. Prisons were unimaginable nightmares; young and old, hard crook and first offender were thrown together to fight for survival. Women were treated even worse than men; hundreds of hardened hookers and murderesses were locked into battle over scant and rotten rations with mothers caught when forced to steal to keep their children from starving. Open sewer trenches for toilets ran through the cells; hundreds jammed together in cells made to hold of score of prisoners; rats and insects were everywhere (quoted from Winkie Pratney, *Revival*, pp. 65–66).

Another writer records of this time that:

> In higher circles of society, people laughed at the mention of religion. Most prominent statesmen were unbe-

lievers and known for grossly immoral lives, drunkenness, and foul language. Marriage was sneered at. Lord Chesterfield's famous letters to educate his son instructed him how to seduce [women]... Church services declined, church buildings fell into disrepair, worship was neglected. Not more than four or five members of the House of Commons attended church (Wesley Duewel, *Revival Fire*, pp. 50–51).

UNITED STATES OF AMERICA: 1730's–1740's

"The habit of the preachers was to address their people as though they were all pious and only needed instruction and confirmation. It was not a common thing to proclaim the terrors of a violated law and insist on the absolute necessity of regeneration." Gilbert Tennent described this preaching: "They often strengthened the hands of the wicked by promising them life. They comfort people before they convince them; sow before they plow: and are busy in raising a fabric before they lay a foundation. These foolish builders strengthen men's carnal security by their soft, selfish, cowardly discourses. They have not the courage or honesty to thrust the nail of terror into the sleeping souls!" (David Smithers, *Gilbert Tennent: Prayer Makes History*).

THE UNITED STATES OF AMERICA: 1790's–1835

"On the heels of the First Great Awakening in America came the French and Indian War (1754–1763), the War of Independence (1775–1783), false French philosophies and widespread infidelity. It was a time of great discouragement for the Church in America. Yet when things seemed the darkest, the fires of revival once again broke forth." Edward

Recognizing the Dance in the Darkness

Dorr Griffin, a Presbyterian minister of the time (b. 1770–d.1837), said:

> As a nation our walls are broken down and our gates are burned. This nation is crumbling from within because the very foundation of the Church has slipped. No longer is Christ alone all-sufficient for all our needs. Jesus has become far less than preeminent among the very ones who claim his name. The brick and mortar of our fleshly methods have failed to repair the spiritual breaches of our walls. How long shall we try in vain to repair our outer walls while God's house of prayer still lies neglected and in ruins? (David Smithers, Edward Griffin: Prayer Makes History).

WALES: 1858–1859

> The Welsh are not supposed to be more addicted to drunkenness than the English, Scotch, or Irish, and yet. . . a vast amount of intemperance existed. Notwithstanding the great efforts made in times past to stem the torrent by means of 'temperance,' and 'total abstinence' societies, drunkenness continued to an alarming extent . . . the generally attendant habit of smoking, absorbed a vast amount of the earnings of the artisan and the labourer; thereby bringing distress and poverty upon themselves and their unhappy families. . . . Drinking had become a snare to young men, who at one time promised well; and very many attribute their backsliding to the indulgence of drinking habits. Multitudes who had taken the 'pledge' of total abstinence had fallen back again into their former courses. . . . It was at this juncture that the revival broke forth; at the time when godly people feared that the tide of intemperance, instead of ebbing, was flowing in more

rapidly (Thomas Phillips, *The Welsh Revival*, pp. 94–95).

During such times, how precious are the words of Isaiah 59:19: "When the enemy comes in like a flood, the Spirit of the LORD will lift up a standard against him."

SOUTH WALES: 1859

"In some places the cause of religion had nearly died away, but now those places are quickened" (Tomas Phillips, *The Welsh Revival*, p. 6).

NORTH WALES: 1859–1860

Baner Cymru, a correspondent at Rhyl, North Wales in 1859 or 1860 wrote:

> "I rejoice to be able to state that the religious awakening so prevalent in other districts has at length reached this place, and the effects by which it is attended prove it to be a visitation from the Lord. The cause of religion in this place was in a depressed state previously; prayer-meetings were announced, but few attended; the ministry was good, but the sermons preached produced but little effect in inducing the hearers to abandon the ways of sin. The church itself was in a sleepy state" (Thomas Phillips, *The Welsh Revival*, pp. 66–67).

NORTHERN IRELAND: 1920's

"In the early 1920's, Northern Ireland passed through a period of great strife and bloodshed. These were times of great despair and apprehension. Fear gripped the heart of many and even spread to the churches and religious community" (David Smithers, *W.P. Nicholson: Prayer Makes History*).

How many characteristics of a dance with darkness did you find from the nine periods of history mentioned above? Compare what you found with my list:

Florence, Italy: Late 1480's
1) Despite being well-educated, people were utterly corrupt.
2) People were given over to entertainment and worldly display. They chased after pleasure and entertainment.
3) People were sexually immoral.
4) People were selfish.
5) They thought little about God.
6) A huge gap existed between the rich and the poor.
7) Common people were the prey of the powerful.
8) Preachers were wicked and fought for political power along with the dukes and kings.

England: 1647
1) Churches were dead, bound in traditions and formalism. They lacked spiritual power.
2) The Church was like the world. The world was more immoral and ungodly because the Church was ungodly.
3) Evil people were content to be evil.
4) Preachers were busy debating each other over fine points of doctrine.
5) Preachers were entangled in politics. (The key word

A Dance in the Dark

here is "entangled").

England: 1660"s to Early 1700's
1) Puritanism (a form of Biblical Christianity) was rejected by England. God's truth found in His word was rejected.
2) England threw off moral restraint.
3) England plunged into godlessness, drunkenness, sexual immorality, and gambling.
4) An "Act of Uniformity" was passed attempting to make all the Churches become uniform. They were all to use the rites and ceremonies found in *The Book of Common Prayer.*
5) Puritans who wanted a purer form of Christianity faced increasing legal hassles because they would not conform.
6) Puritans became a thorn in the side of the state church, which was backed by the government.
7) Ministers who would not conform to the Act of Uniformity were removed from their churches and forbidden to preach.
8) Some of them were thrown in prison. Some died there.
9) A vicious thought war against supernatural Christianity began. People sought to rationalize the Bible, the Virgin Birth, and other miracles.
10) Deism, a false belief system that said human reason and not divine revelation was the way to find morality and truth, arose in the land, challenging the tenets of Christianity.

11) Churches were cold and formal.
12) Alcohol gripped and destroyed many families.
13) Entertainment was gruesome and bloody. People of all ages gathered to watch daily hangings.
14) Prisons were deplorable.
15) People laughed and scoffed at religion (Christianity).
16) Politicians were unbelievers and led grossly immoral lives. One leading politician even taught his sons how to seduce women.
17) Marriage was mocked.
18) Church services declined and church buildings fell into disrepair.

The United States of America: 1730's to 1740's
1) Preachers did not preach the demands of the Law of God.
2) Preachers treated everyone as though they were pious.
3) Preachers did not insist that people needed to be born again.
4) Preachers promised people security in God without confronting their sin.

The United States of America: 1790's to 1835
1) False French philosophies from the Enlightenment were leading people astray, replacing true faith with lies.
2) There was widespread infidelity and immorality.
3) Jesus was not the center of church life.

4) The Church was powerless against the culture.

Wales: 1858–1859
1) Drunkenness was rampant.
2) All efforts to stem the tide of the destruction of drunkenness were futile. The Church had no power against it.
3) Drinking alcoholic beverages and smoking consumed people's wealth and brought families into poverty.
4) Young Christian men backslid into the arms of alcohol.

South Wales: 1859
1) The Christian faith almost died out.

North Wales: 1859–1860
1) Religion (Christianity) was in a depressed state. Prayer meetings were announced, but few attended them.
2) Preaching produced little effect in causing people to abandon sin.
3) The Church was in a sleepy state.

Northern Ireland: 1920's
1) Great strife and bloodshed was in the land.
2) There was much despair and apprehension in the land.
3) Fear gripped the heart of many, including those in the Church.

Recognizing the Dance in the Darkness

Many of the characteristics of a dance with darkness can be seen in the headlines and news articles of our day in our nation.

- Consider the above nine periods of history.
- Did you notice the patterns of darkness found in them?
- Thinking of our own time and what we see in the daily news, can you notice the darkness as it is closing in?

UNITED STATES OF AMERICA: 2000–2016

It doesn't take much effort to see the description of England from the late 1600's and the early 1700's reflected in *our* time and in *our* nation. I am going to quote Dallimore's description of England again, but I am going to alter it a bit so we can see how pertinent this really is to our time. Listen to the voice of the Holy Spirit as you read this.

"In the violent rejection of Biblical Christianity that accompanies the ascension to power of a certain political and academic mind-set, much of this nation is throwing off restraint and plunging into godlessness, drunkenness, drug addiction, sexual immorality sexual perversion, and gambling due to the legalization of it all by certain politicians and the pushing of it by academia. Biblical Christianity is becoming a thorn in the side of the state, the decadent educational system, and the apostate church. Those who believe the Word of God are beginning to face increasing legal hassles. The ministers and followers of Christ who refuse to submit to the legalization of abortion and the legalization of homosexuality and perversion will be ejected from their churches and forbidden to preach the truth under severe penalty of law. Many will be imprisoned and suffer and die. Deism and Darwinism, the rejection of the supernatural power of God, has already infiltrated our schools, our seats of government, our homes, and our legal system. A vicious thought-war against supernatural Christianity is raging in the land. There is an attempt to silence anybody who believes the truth of the Word of God and would dare to oppose the ungodliness rampant in the Church and in the land. The dead formalism of the American church and the absence of the fire of God and brokenness in the pulpit and the hypocrisy of many in the ministry are driving people from the churches. Many are coming to the conclusion that Christianity is not real. The drug addiction craze is turning houses and neighborhoods everywhere into drug shops and funeral parlors. The spiraling economic dilemma and taxes are making the poor poorer. The drug addiction and increasing demon possession are turning people into what they never were before—cruel and inhuman. Our schools and neighborhoods are not safe. Children are murdering children. And the answer does not lie in a political solution."

CHAPTER SIX

THE RAY OF HOPE—
AFTER DARKNESS, LIGHT

The material in the previous pages shows that there have been many periods of darkness in history. No matter how deep a culture's dance in the darkness is, there is a ray of hope. All of the dark periods mentioned above were followed by a period of revival.

The character of God militates against the darkness. Our very first encounter with God in the pages of Holy Scripture shows Him working to dispel the darkness and to bring light. "The earth was without form, and void; and darkness was on the face of the deep. And the Spirit of God was hovering over the face of the waters. Then God said, "Let there be light; and there was light" (Genesis 1:2–3). Even the account of the progression of each day of creation proceeds from darkness to light. For example, "So the evening and the morning were the first day" (Genesis 1:5). This pattern is consistent throughout the creation account. God never allows darkness to ultimately triumph. "And the light shines in the darkness, and the darkness did not compre-

A Dance in the Dark

hend [apprehend] it" (John 1:5). The greatest example of God's fighting against the darkness is found at Golgotha's hill. On the old rugged cross God dealt the death blow to the kingdom of darkness. In the resurrection of Christ Jesus triumph was proclaimed. That victory has been working itself out in revivals throughout history. R. C. Sproul points out the motto of the Protestant Reformation: *Post tenebras lux*: "After darkness, light" (Archie Parrish and R.C. Sproul, *The Spirit of Revival*, p. 17). Scripture and revival history give us the magnificent story of God's battling against the darkness.

Revival

When God steps down into history and turns back the advancing powers of darkness, revival occurs. People ask, "What is revival?" Richard Owen Roberts points out the difficulty in pinning down a definition. He states, "Is it not immediately apparent that in using the term *revival* one runs the risk of being misunderstood? What revival means to a Southerner may be different from what a Northeasterner has in mind. A European's concept of revival may be altogether different from that of an American" (Richard Owen Roberts, *Revival*, p. 15). Nevertheless we must attempt to define the term.

Often the starting point is to define what something is not. Revival is not a series of meetings that have been scheduled, though there may be meetings. Revival is not the carrying out of church growth plans. Revival is not swinging from the chandeliers during a church service. Revival is not something that man does.

The Ray of Hope—After Darkness, Light

The best way of defining revival may be by describing it. Revival is when the Church awakens from its slumber. Revival is when God comes in such power that a tangible presence can be felt everywhere. Revival is when the awareness of our separation from God is so real that business as usual comes to a screeching halt. Revival is when Christians and sinners alike are on their faces under deep conviction of sin against a holy God. Revival is when the burden to pray for the powerless Church and for the lost and dying world drives us to our knees. In the words of Wesley Duewel, "God's presence and power are so mightily and extensively at work during revival that God accomplishes more in hours or days than usually results from years of faithful nonrevival ministry. Revival usually involves some preaching and evangelism. But revival is far more than evangelism. Man can evangelize, only God can give revival" (Duewel, *Revival Fire*, p. 11). Duncan Campbell, in his sermon "When the Mountains Flowed Down," defined revival in these words:

> First, let me tell you what I mean by revival. In an evangelistic campaign or crusade, there will be hundreds or even thousands of people making decisions for Jesus Christ, but the community remains untouched, and the churches continue much the same as before the outreach. In revival, God moves in the district. Suddenly, the community becomes God conscious. The Spirit of God grips men and women in such a way that even work is given up as people give themselves to waiting upon God. In the midst of the Lewis awakening, the parish minister at Barvas wrote, "The Spirit of the Lord was

resting on meadow and moorland, and even on the public roads." This presence of God is the supreme characteristic of a God-sent revival. Of the hundreds who found Jesus Christ during this time fully seventy-five percent were saved before they came near a meeting or heard a sermon by myself or any other ministers in the parish. The power of God, the Spirit of God, was moving in operation, and the fear of God gripped the souls of men. This is God-sent revival as distinct from special efforts in the field of evangelism.

To quote Richard Owen Roberts: "In using the term *revival*, I am speaking of an *extraordinary movement of the Holy Spirit producing extraordinary results*" (*Revival*, p. 16). In a period of darkness and decline, evil is called good and good is called evil. Revival is when everything that God's Word calls darkness and evil begins to be viewed as the evil that it is. It is when the good that has been called evil begins to be seen as the good that it is. Everything gets turned right side up.

STAGES OUT OF THE DARKNESS

Just as there are steps or patterns into the darkness, there are steps or patterns that mark the road out of the darkness. It is not the purpose of this book to discuss this in detail. However, Richard Owen Roberts gives the following general overview or pattern that leads from the darkness to the light (Richard Owen Roberts, *The Solemn Assembly*). The following is a condensed paraphrase:

1) A tragic declension occurs: Every revival in the Old Testament was preceded by moral and spiritual decline.

2) A righteous judgment from God comes. Without exception, Old Testament revivals were preceded by God's judgment. The first type of judgment was a remedial judgment. This judgment was meant to instruct the people in the error of their ways. God might send more than one remedial judgment. If the remedial judgments are ignored, a final judgment comes.
3) God raises up an immensely burdened leader or leaders.
4) Some extraordinary action is taken. Usually it is a solemn assembly with prayer and repentance.

GOD STEPS DOWN

In response to such an extraordinary action, God has often stepped down to drive back the darkness. This intervention of God has been described by several people in different ways. It is often described as God accomplishing more in a short period of time than all the efforts of preachers and missionaries over long periods of time. Here are some recorded statements from different writers about several such times.

At Montgomeryshire, Wales in 1859 a correspondent of the *Drysorfa* reported, "I have never witnessed anything like that which I see daily. You hear of nothing but the revival. Ungodly people quake and tremble. God, in His grace, has done more within the last fortnight in this part of the country than had been accomplished for an age previously" (Thomas Philips, *The Welsh Revival*, p. 60).

Dennis F. Kinlaw, a past president of Asbury College,

A Dance in the Dark

once said, "Give me one divine moment when God acts and I say that moment is far superior to all the human efforts of man throughout the centuries" (Robert Coleman, ed., *One Divine Moment: The Asbury Revival*, p. 5).

I have not been able to verify where the following quote came from (it might even be my own), but it is too important to ignore. "There must arise within the hearts of Christians across this land a pleading, a longing, a crying out to God to send one divine moment when God acts in order to change the hearts of the people of this nation. That one divine moment will accomplish more than all of the Christian conferences, evangelistic crusades and efforts of the past forty years."

J. Philip Hogan, executive director of the Division of Foreign Missions for the Assemblies of God, was speaking about a divine moment from God that came to the country of Argentina when he said, "Such an outpouring and development is now in force in Argentina, an indigenous move of God's Spirit so engulfing that it overwhelms all previous effort in evangelism and church planting in that country" (Colin C. Whittaker, *Great Revivals*, p. 9).

J. Gilchrist Lawson said in his book *Deeper Experiences of Famous Christians*, "The Holy Spirit can teach men more about Christ in one hour than the greatest preacher can teach them in fifty or even in a hundred years without the Spirit enlightening them" (p. 36).

Consider again Wesley Duewel's statement, in his introduction to *Revival Fire*, "God's presence and power are so mightily and extensively at work during revival that God accomplishes more in hours or days than usually results

The Ray of Hope—After Darkness, Light

from years of faithful nonrevival ministry" (p. 11).

During the South African Revival during the 1860's, "At Wellington a Christian had prayed for weeks for revival and had organized prayer meetings. God worked so mightily that the church consistory declared that God had accomplished more in a few weeks than in all the previous history of the church" (Duewel, *Revival Fire*, p. 174).

GOD'S WILLINGNESS

The evidence is overwhelming that God is willing to send one divine moment to transform nations and cultures. These divine moments have consistent patterns. There have been many such moves of God's Spirit in history. It is my intent to show in future books what has happened to bring about such moves of God's Spirit and what they look like. How do you recognize when God's Spirit is moving? Just as there were patterns to a dance in the darkness, there are patterns to moves into the light. It is also my intent to speak about the dangers connected with them. Regardless of the dangers, we must have such a move of God's Spirit if our nation is to survive. Would you join me in crying out to God for such a divine moment? If your heart shouts "Yes!" then as you read the prayer in the next chapter, let it become your prayer as well.

CHAPTER SEVEN

"ONE DIVINE MOMENT" A PRAYER: MY HEART'S CRY

God, give us another divine moment that will do more to civilize and alter the harmful politics of this nation than all of our efforts by elections to put into political office those who have a fear of the one true God. Give us one divine moment when the Spirit of God so grips the hearts of the Church in this land that she will fall on her face in repentance and deep sorrow for our sins against the God who has loved us so. Give us one divine moment to halt our plummet into the abyss of sin, one divine moment to snatch from hell those who are held captive by Satan's grasp, one divine moment when all the naysayers will stand in awe before Almighty God. Give us one divine moment when all the demons of hell will tremble at the presence of our King Jesus, the King of kings and the LORD of Lords. Give us one divine moment when all the traps and snares that Satan has set for the people of God in this land will divide and part like the parting of the Red Sea when God's children escaped from Pharaoh's clutches. Give us one divine moment before our eyes close in death so that like Simeon of old we can cry, "Lord, now You are letting Your servant depart in peace . . . for my eyes have seen Your salvation" (Luke 2:29–30). Give us one divine moment so that we may behold the deliverance of God for our nation. Give us one divine moment when the blinders are ripped from the eyes of those who know not what they do and the glorious light of the gospel shines into their souls and they fall on their faces in surrender to the Lord Jesus Christ. Give us one divine moment! Give me one divine moment or let me die!

Will you join me in continuing to seek God for one more divine moment to bring us out of this horrible dance of doom in the darkness?

POSTLUDE

THE BURDEN

Greetings in the name of the King,

If you are reading this postlude, it is perhaps because you felt your heart resonate with the sentiments of this book or perhaps with the prayer in the previous chapter. I believe God asked me to "Write the vision and make it plain . . . that he may run who reads it" (Habakkuk 2:2). What is on my heart is more like a burden than a vision. My heart is heavy for America. The sins of our nation have reached to the highest heaven. The sins of the church in America have brought about its powerlessness. Much of what is passing as the power of God is a charade. The hour is late, and God is calling the Church in America to "Repent therefore and be converted [turned], that your sins may be blotted out, so that times of refreshing may come from the presence of the Lord" (Acts 3:19).

We must have an awakening from God. The problems we are facing as a nation are beyond the ability of the politicians to solve them. The poverty in our land is growing. The fear of terrorism lurks in the hearts of young and old alike. Fewer people are becoming true followers of the Lord

A Dance in the Dark

Jesus Christ in our land. Many churches are embracing doctrines that are strange fire upon the altar of God. Does your heart cry as mine does with the prophet Habakkuk, "O LORD, how long shall I cry, and You will not hear?" (Habakkuk 1:2). When I see the calamities in our land, the floods, the whirlwinds, the pursuit of false gods, all because we have forsaken the living God, I also cry with Habakkuk, "O LORD, I have heard your speech and was afraid; O LORD revive your work in the midst of the years! In the midst of the years make it known; in wrath remember mercy" (Habakkuk 3:2).

We are in desperate need of a time of refreshing. Some would say, "What we need is a habitation, not a visitation." But I would rather have a visitation from God than nothing at all. We need what Duncan Campbell called "God-sent revival."

God has left memorial stones of His faithfulness all across this nation and across the world, but Satan has done a good job of burying them. I have read about great moves of God and then sought to go where they had transpired. Sometimes I go to the graveside of the person God had used in that awakening or visit the region or building that housed a move in the past and as a touch point for prayer ask God to do it again. Invariably I have divine appointments to help me find what I am looking for.

Out of this time of seeking and reading, God birthed this and other materials. We can know much about how God has moved in the past and also about what has either opened up or obstructed revival. Perhaps your heart, like mine, is burdened for God to do something that only He

Postlude: The Burden

can get credit for, and you are seeking God for the time of refreshing that the Church in America must have or perish! Let us clasp hands and grab the horns of the altar and seek God until He rains righteousness upon us.

Seeking His face for the land I love, in the service of Christ the King,

B. J. Isaacs

Bibliography

Campbell, Duncan. "When the Mountains Flowed Down." http://www.revival-library.org/index.php/catalogues-menu/20th-century/ when-the-mountains-floweddown

Coleman, Robert E., ed. *One Divine Moment: The Asbury Revival*. Old Tappan, NJ: Fleming H. Revell, 1970.

Duewel, Wesley. *Revival Fire*. Grand Rapids, MI: Zondervan, 1995.

Lawson, James Gilchrist. *Deeper Experiences of Famous Christians*. Anderson, IN: Warner Press, 1911.

Mataxas, Eric. *Bonhoeffer: Pastor, Martyr, Prophet, Spy*. Nashville: Thomas Nelson, 2010.

Parrish, Archie and R.C. Sproul, *The Spirit of Revival: Discovering the Wisdom of Jonathan Edwards*. Wheaton, IL: Crossway, 2000.

Phillips, Thomas. *The Welsh Revival: Its Origin and Development*. Edinburgh, Scotland and Pittsburgh, PA: The Banner of Truth Trust, 1998 reprint (originally published in 1860).

Pratney, Winkie. *Revival*. Springdale, PA: Whitaker House, 1983.

Roberts, Richard Owen. *Revival*. Wheaton, IL: Richard Owen Roberts Publishers, 1993.

_____. *The Solemn Assembly*. Wheaton, IL: International Awakening Press, 1989.

Smithers, David. "Richard Baxter: Prayer Makes History." http://articles.ochristian.com/preacher164-1.shtml.

_____. "George Fox: Prayer Makes History." http://articles.ochristian.com/preacher164-1.shtml.

_____. "Edward Griffin: Prayer Makes History." http://articles.ochristian.com/preacher164-1.shtml.

_____. "W.P. Nicholson: Prayer Makes History." http://articles.ochristian.com/preacher164-1.shtml.

_____. "Girolamo Savonarola: Prayer Makes History." http://articles.ochristian.com/preacher164-1.shtml.

_____. "Gilbert Tennent: Prayer Makes History." http://articles.ochristian.com/preacher164-1.shtml.

Whittaker, Colin C. *Great Revivals*. Springfield, MO: Gospel Publishing House, 1984.

About the Author

B.J. Isaacs has been serving the Lord for over forty years with a passion to see the lost come to Jesus and for God's Kingdom purposes to be established on the earth. He has served in various positions at pastoral and ministerial levels, fellowshipped in several denominations, pioneered an interdenominational church, and taught in several schools ranging from junior high through Bible college. He has enjoyed the privilege of participating in several short term mission trips both in the USA and in Jamaica, Haiti, and Honduras. He has carried the gospel from the public square to prison, from "champa" to mission, from pulpit to house church, from gospel tent to the streets.

He was born in central Illinois, raised at Buckner Baptist Orphanage (a.k.a. Buckner Baptist Children's Home) in Dallas, Texas, and returned to Illinois while a teenager. As an emancipated minor, he completed high school in Sullivan, Illinois and subsequently enlisted in the army, serving in Vietnam. Although he knew of the Lord and showed evidence of being called to preach as a young boy, he walked away from all of this until his life fell apart with a

A Dance in the Dark

divorce, failing grades in pharmacy, and dabbling in the occult. When confronted with the question of whether to serve God or the devil, he surrendered his life to the Lord in 1977. *(His testimony has been aired on the radio show "Unshackled" by Pacific Garden Mission in Chicago, Illinois.)* Since then, he has served as a volunteer chaplain at a mental health center in the Chicago area, as a counselor at Pacific Garden Mission, pastored two churches in the state of Georgia, taught in Christian schools, been a traveling evangelist, a professor of Greek, an associate pastor of a Foursquare Church in Parma, Ohio, and pioneered a church in Cleveland, Ohio, as well as interim pastoral positions. Currently he is part of the North East Ohio House Church Network.

He and his wife, Bonnie, are parents of three daughters and two sons-in-law. He holds a bachelor's degree from Concordia Lutheran College and a Master of Arts in Theological Studies from Northern Baptist Theological Seminary. Yet, B.J. feels that all these accomplishments are as nothing in comparison to the most vital task that God has ever burdened his heart with… that of carrying forth the message of our desperate and urgent need for revival. His soul cries out to God as did the Prophet Isaiah **"Oh, that You would rend the heavens! That You would come down!" (Isaiah 64:1).**

If God has pricked your heart as you have read this book and you feel the Lord is asking you to contact me, please reach out to me at:

<u>onedivinemoment@gmail.com</u>

As the Lord directs, perhaps we can meet and I can share more about this subject with you and/or your church group. The Lord laid on my heart to begin small and make my research findings available in segments to those who are asking to learn more. This book is Book One of *Revival: The Consistency of God*. In Book Two we will be looking at the twilight in which there is a move out of darkness into the light. If you would like to be notified of additional publications, I would be happy to get back to you as these become available.

For additional information, you might visit our website at:

www.ReviveUsOhGod.com

CPSIA information can be obtained
at www.ICGtesting.com
Printed in the USA
BVHW04s1151050718
520879BV00011B/70/P